T0082796

THE *Flower* OUTSIDE THE *Garden*

Corbin Wood

THE FLOWER OUTSIDE THE GARDEN

iUniverse books may be ordered through booksellers or by contacting:

iUniverse
1663 Liberty Drive
Bloomington, IN 47403
www.iuniverse.com
844-349-9409

Because of the dynamic nature of the Internet, any web addresses or links contained in this book may have changed since publication and may no longer be valid. The views expressed in this work are solely those of the author and do not necessarily reflect the views of the publisher, and the publisher hereby disclaims any responsibility for them.

Any people depicted in stock imagery provided by Getty Images are models, and such images are being used for illustrative purposes only. Certain stock imagery © Getty Images.

ISBN: 978-1-6632-1727-1 (sc)
ISBN: 978-1-6632-1682-3 (e)

Library of Congress Control Number: 2021901452

Print information available on the last page.

iUniverse rev. date: 01/27/2021

Composed for the individual, the meant-well,

    The introvert, the rebel, the stand alone,

The proud, the deeply rooted, the realist,

    The optimist, the pessimist, the brave,

Most of all composed for the flower outside the garden.

I saw the way you looked at me,

As if you were looking at forever.

Only to my surprise

Were you looking past me.

It felt like home,

It felt like comfort.

Not realizing I was sitting next to the AC unit

In a burning building.

There is a calm to not knowing why,

Even more so than knowing why.

Everything you said, I listened to.

Everything I said, you listened to.

The only difference was I took it to heart;

You took it for granted.

I watched you question your decisions,

Countless hours, mentally exhausted.

Finding every answer led to another question

What beauty you showed.

Even in the darkest hours, your light guided me home

What a ride it was,

Our ups and downs, the twists and turns,

Only to get off before the excitement set in.

The thing about being blind to love

Is you never see the end coming.

We latched on to one another

Like two orphans looking for hope,

A life we could not battle alone,

A war we could not win apart.

To pray for rain is to accept the clouds,

For they too provide a purpose.

The sun is too vibrant to see you cry.

I would be lying if I said I did not think of you.

It is simply better comprising

With the truth unspoken.

We grew together

Only to find out we were rooted in different soils.

I excused myself from your table.

The company was just too disillusioned with the world.

The city lights lined the sidewalk of your street,

Leading in one direction back to your place,

And in the other the future that was to come without you.

I fell in love with the smallest of features of you.

Everything you felt that went unnoticed was magnified.

It is admired; it is beauty; most importantly it is loved.

It's not so much the distance now that hurts the most,

As it is the memories of how close we used to be.

Never stop loving;

One day you will too have your love.

I have watched dysfunctional relationships.

I have seen bitter endings.

I have seen pain and hurt and long nights.

I have heard stories of disconnect and regret.

On the other hand, I have heard of happiness.

I have seen positivity and growth.

I have had the pleasure of watching people flourish in love.

Which comes to show that love is the most

powerful drug known to humankind.

I am unimpressed with small talk;

It does me no good to sit on the surface,

For the only real conversations we have are

when we let ourselves become vulnerable.

I have been involved in all types of relationships—

Young and dreaming,

Short and to the point,

Dragging and draining—

Each showing me a different level of love

And the realization that I jump into each

with no intentions of landing.

Flying was always the best part.

I knew you were the one

When this gypsy soul no longer wanted to run.

There will always be that one person

you will have to thank.

Thank them for their time.

Thank them for their effort.

Thank them for their lessons.

More importantly, thank them for your growth,

For without your thanks, you would

forever be you're welcome.

I could never be grateful enough for your patience,

All the room you gave me to make

mistakes and learn from them.

You helped me be self-sufficient, and

for that I owe you everything.

When I ask you what brings you happiness,

What brings you sadness,

What brings you anxiety,

What brings you relief,

Is it shameful to say you can immediately think

of one thing or person that matches all?

The premise in which you show up to

something is strangely satisfying,

Whether you were invited or felt you invited yourself.

It makes no difference.

You realize that you're detoxifying in both situations.

You make the conscious decision to wake
up every day and direct your mood.
It is no other's responsibility but your
own to shine your own light.
Even a lamp with a shade still shines because
the bulb switch was turned on.

Do we place too much interest on physical comparisons?

Is it the human design to admire physical attributes

When the strongest parts of you

Are not physical?

When the allure of physicality in relationships dissolves,

Will you have enough elsewhere to watch it evolve?

I loved you for all your curves,

All your marks.

I loved you even more

For the way you loved mine.

Not perfection, but you sure made me feel like it.

You cannot expect all your advice to be

received how you want it to be.

Do not be emotional in your advice.

Whether you have been through it yourself or not,

It's not up to you to decide how to take it.

I never judged you for your mistakes.

I only judged you

For the way you judged yourself when you made them.

It is foolish to think it's not scary to

reveal your true self to others,

But I promise it's much worse never giving

yourself the chance to do so.

In the walk of life, there is never a misstep,

Just a new direction.

May your joy be everlasting

And your pain brief.

Appreciate both,

For one means nothing

Without the other.

Make sure you give yourself the credit

You deserve daily

For your life.

In every circumstance, it is your most beautiful work.

I think people misconstrue being cordial.

I can feel slighted and still wish you nothing but the best.

When you put so much focus on making others happy,

You do nothing but relinquish your

power to make yourself happy.

You learn happiness is not always

given in equal reciprocation.

When you start with yourself,

You learn how to give out the correct amount.

Happiness hydrates in the right measurement:

Too little, you thirst; too much, you drown.

Please do not let me become comfortable.

Once you let me do so,

You will lose me forever.

I have made decisions knowing the outcome

before I even decided to act.

Usually those end up being my worse decisions.

I made them because you always think there

is the possibility it will end differently.

I always appreciated the peacefulness of being alone.

It was the only time I could escape

the calamity that was you.

It hurts,

Getting caught in your own fantasy.

You overthink, embellish, and live

in the memory of what-ifs.

What if everything went how you planned?

Even then, would you still be happy?

Tattoo lover,

Like the ink drawn into your skin.

The pain of becoming attached to you

Was worth the time.

Seeing eye to eye was never easy.

Arguing, however, ended up being the

only time I got to see your eyes.

Sometimes I wish we would fight all night.

There is nothing wrong with sharing

your heart with all you meet.

Just realize

It will not be received the same by everyone.

Our drunken nights lead to sobering love,

Because even when I lose control,

you always bring me back.

Appreciate the unspoken love you receive.
Words can evaporate as quickly as they
remove themselves from the lips.

Forgiven—

It's easy to forgive others, harder to forgive yourself.

I want to get you

Naked, remove your

Fears, your sadness, your

Mind's calamity, only

To help you dress

In your own

Comfort.

I need space;

Take what you need.

Expecting to return in the same

Location will only leave you standing

Alone.

SJ

Printed in the United States
By Bookmasters